ai

Snake is talking to Bee, but she doesn't hear him. She puts her hand behind her ear and says *ai?* Snake tells her she should say *pardon.*

Action: Cup your hand over your ear as if you are trying to hear something, and say *ai?*

Trace over the dotted lines.

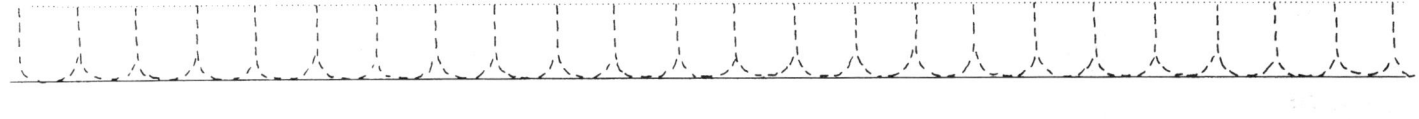

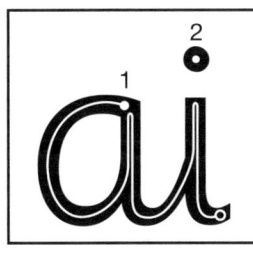 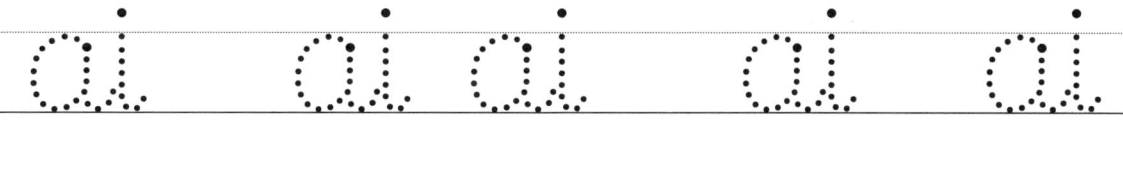

rain

train

tail

snail

J j

Snake joins in the fun with Inky and pretends he is wobbling like jelly on a plate, saying *j, j, j, j*.

Action: Pretend to wobble like jelly on a plate, saying *j, j, j, j*.

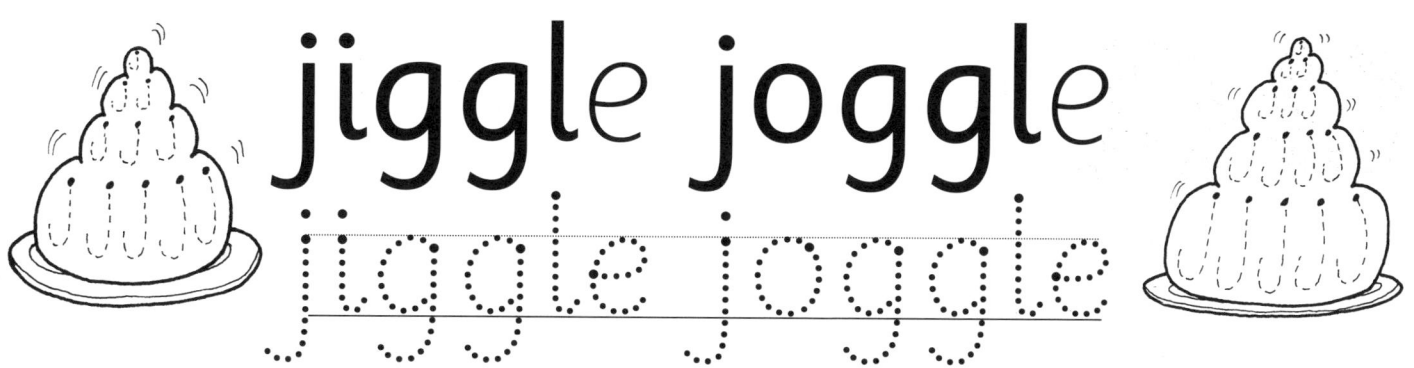

jiggle joggle
jiggle joggle

Note: The ‹e› is silent here in 'jiggle' and 'joggle', so it is shown in faint type.

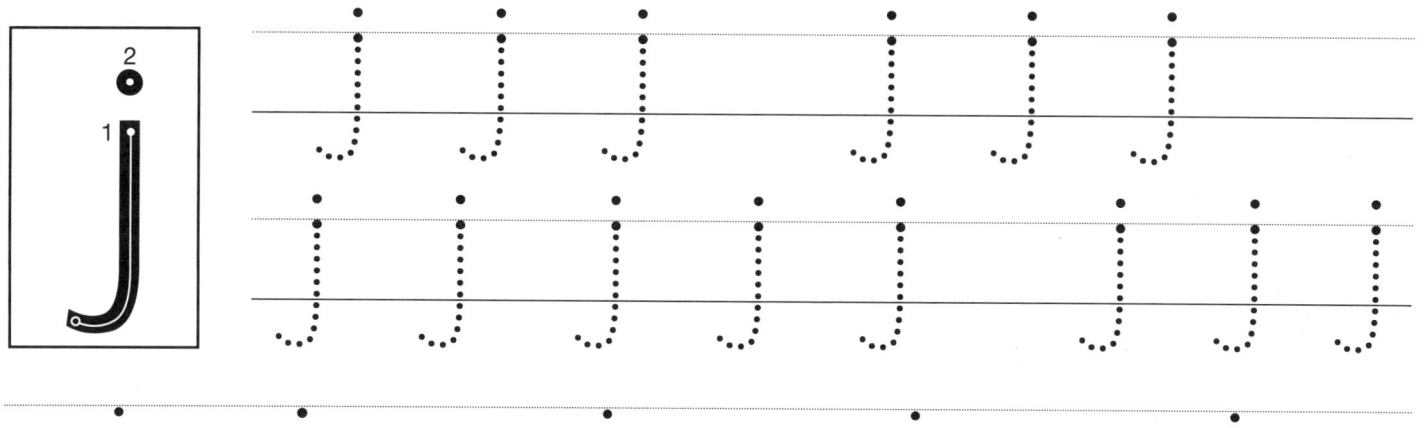

jacket

jam

juggle

jump

oa

A big oak tree has fallen on the poor old goat. When Bee and Inky see what has happened, they say *oa!*

Action: Bring your hand over your mouth as if something has gone wrong, and say *oa!*

Trace the dotted lines to make the pattern.

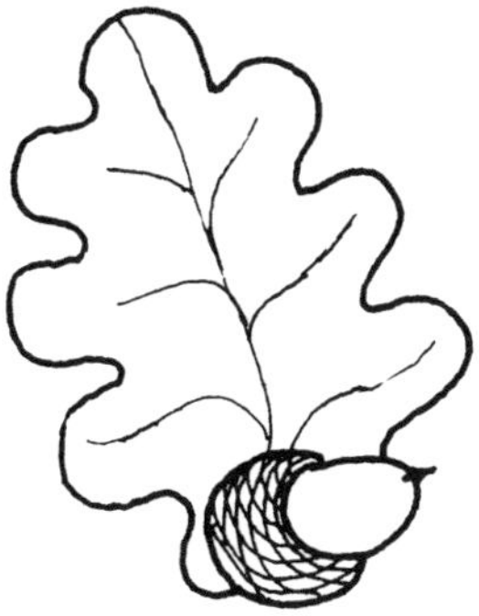

oa oa goat

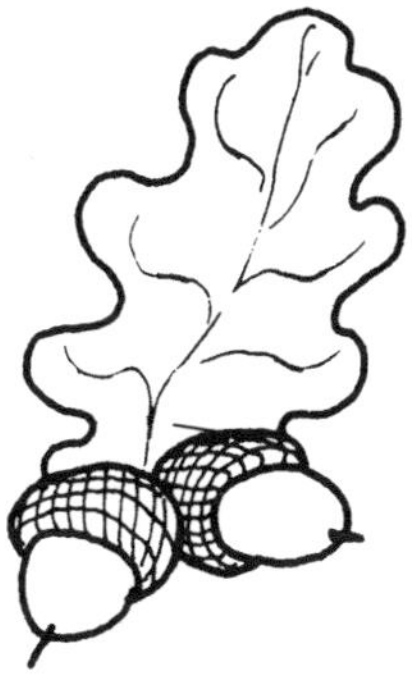

oa oa oa oa
oa oa oa

oak
soap
goat
boat

ie

A boy is going to a party as a sailor. As he is getting ready, he salutes and says *ie, ie!*

Action: Salute as if you are a sailor, saying *ie-ie*.

Trace over the dotted lines.

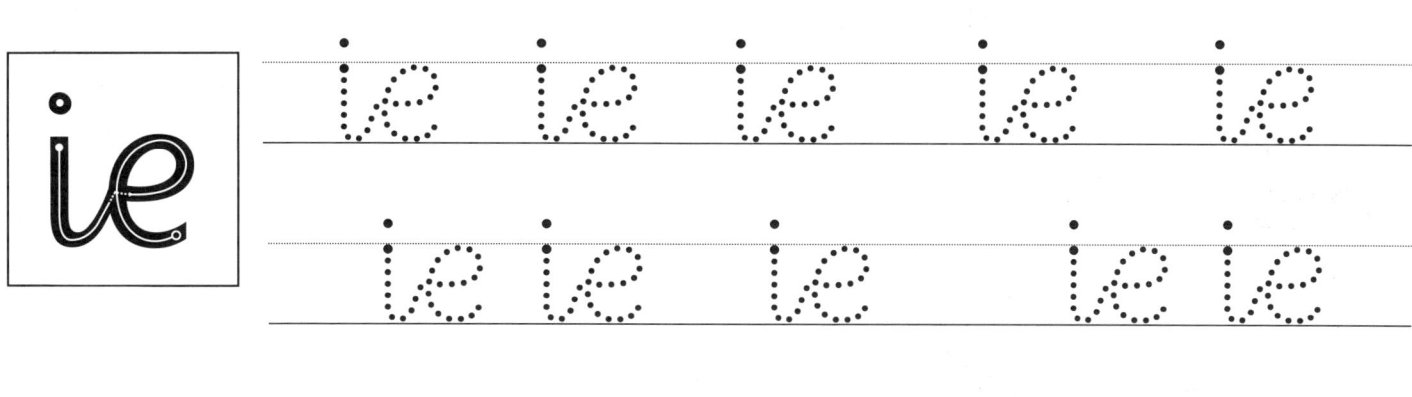

pie

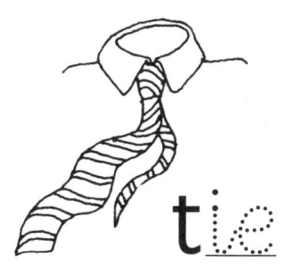

tie

flies

magpie

ee or

Snake and Inky know a very friendly donkey. Whenever he sees anyone, he waggles his ears and calls *ee or! ee or!*

Action: Put your hands on your head like a donkey's ears. Point them up for *ee* and down for *or*.

ee or   ee or

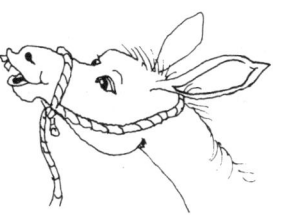

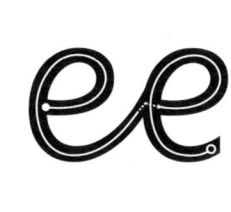
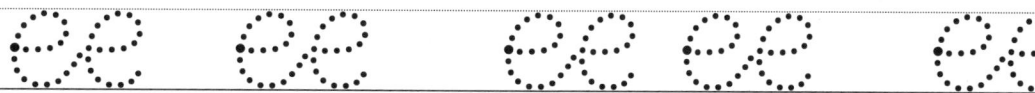
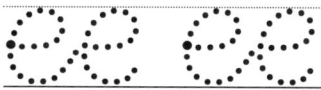

b<u>ee</u>   f<u>ee</u>t   tr<u>ee</u>

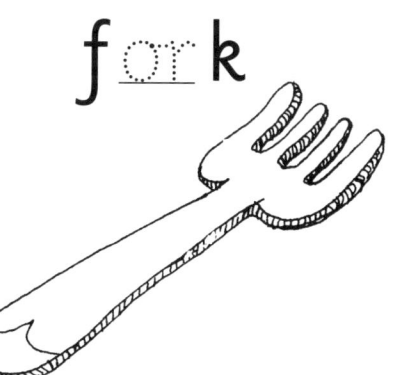

st<u>or</u>m   f<u>or</u>k   h<u>or</u>se

11

Look at each picture and listen for the sounds in the word. Then write the letters for the sounds and read the word.

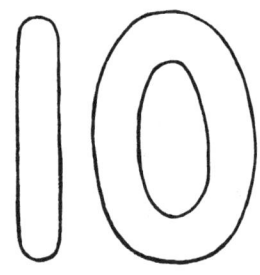

___ ___ ___   ___ ___ ___   ___ ___ ___

___ ___ ___   ___ ___ ___   ___ ___ ___

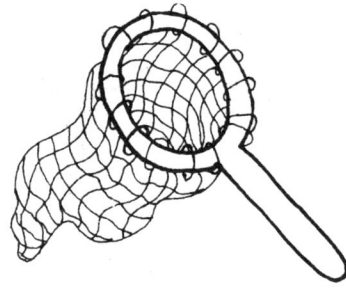

___ ___ ___   ___ ___ ___   ___ ___ ___

Each dot represents one sound. For each word, point to the dots, say the sounds and listen for the word. Then draw a picture.

Read the phrases and match each one to its picture.

a big train

a green frog

a nest and eggs

an oak tree

ducks on a pond

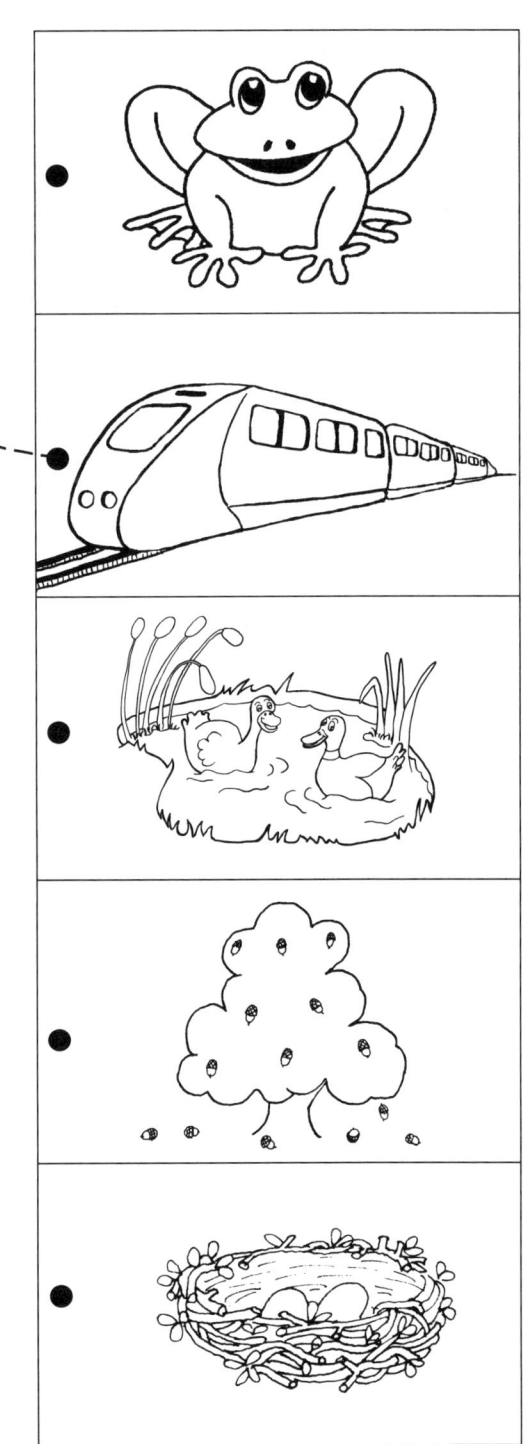

Anagrams

Say the words, listen for the sounds and write the words.

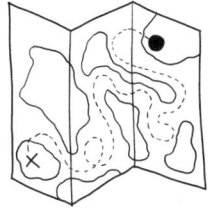 p m a

 o l g

 n p e

 e n t s

 l l i h

 p n o d

 a i r n

 r e e t

 t c o a

Practise the ‹c› shape and make waves in the sea. Starting at the dots, take your pencil over to form the top of the ‹c›, then stop and come back around. The letters ‹a, d, o, g, q› are all written by starting with a ‹c› shape.

Join each picture to its digraph.

Write, read and draw a picture.

Join each picture to its digraph.

Fill in the letters and read the words.

Read the words, then join each word to its picture.

Say the word for each picture and listen for the sounds. Then write the letters for the sounds and read the word.

ai ee ie oa

Count the spiders.

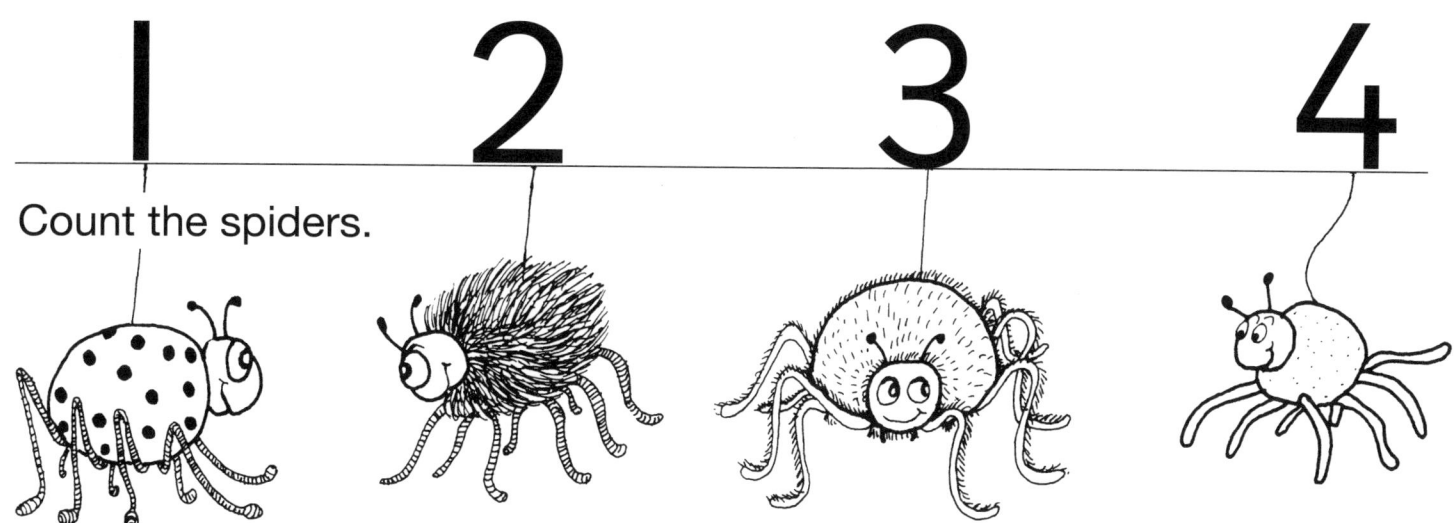

Trace over the dotted lines to write the number 4.

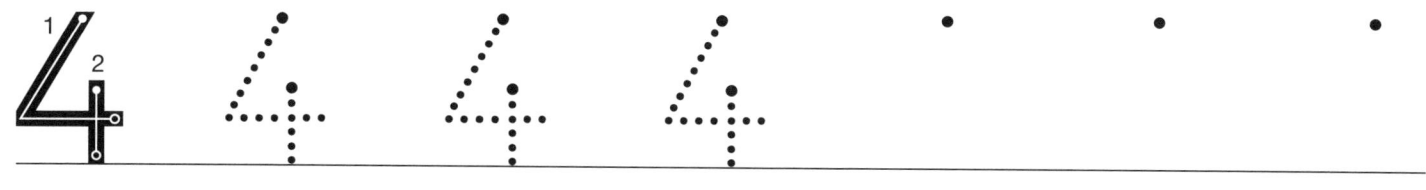

Find the 4 spiders.

Activity

Make some multicoloured jelly

Make some jelly in the first colour and leave it to set at the bottom of the mould. Then repeat with two other colours, leaving each colour to cool a little before adding it to the mould. When set, turn the jelly out and watch it wobble!

Raindrops

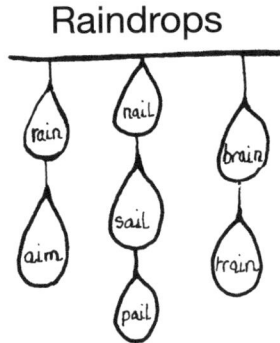

String together some paper raindrops.

Write /ai/ words on them, such as *rain, sail, train, brain*.

Make your own vowel forest

Play I-Spy

Choose an object you can see and say 'I spy, with my little eye, something beginning with /t/' (for example). The others look for things beginning with that sound and guess the answer. Vary the game by saying 'something *ending* with…'.

Make a wall poster of the vowel forest. Cut out four big tree shapes and stick them on a large piece of paper. Collect words and pictures that use the long vowel sounds /ai, ee, ie, oa/, and stick them on the correct trees. (Keep a space for the /ue/ tree activity in Workbook 7.)